Lizzie S.] [from old catalog] [Patten

Wax flowers and fruit modeling without a teacher

a practical treatise on the art of modeling and coloring wax, so as to

imitate almost any kind of flower or fruit

Lizzie S.] [from old catalog] [Patten

Wax flowers and fruit modeling without a teacher
a practical treatise on the art of modeling and coloring wax, so as to imitate almost any kind of flower or fruit

ISBN/EAN: 9783744739108

Printed in Europe, USA, Canada, Australia, Japan

Cover: Foto ©Lupo / pixelio.de

More available books at **www.hansebooks.com**

WAX FLOWERS

—— AND ——

Fruit Modeling

WITHOUT A TEACHER.

WITH ILLUSTRATIONS.

A PRACTICAL TREATISE ON THE ART OF MODELING AND
COLORING WAX, SO AS TO IMITATE ALMOST
ANY KIND OF FLOWER OR FRUIT.

ALSO,

Teaches How to Make Wax Leaves, Crosses, &c.

New York:

J. L. PATTEN & CO., PUBLISHERS,

162 WILLIAM STREET.

1876.

THE ART

OF

MODELING FLOWERS IN WAX.

THE art of modeling flowers in wax was formerly considered very difficult, but great improvements have recently been made, and the system is now reduced to great simplicity; and my object in writing this little manual is to place this beautiful art within the reach of all, so that any person of taste and ingenuity, will be able, after a little practice, to imitate faithfully any flower they may choose.

I would urge beginners to commence with some simple flower, one of simple construction and coloring; they will thus become accustomed to handling the wax—to the use of the modeling pin—and it will then be easier to imitate flowers requiring greater skill in handling.

It will be necessary to have the wax of different degrees of thickness, as some flowers require much thicker wax than others. The double or thick wax is used for such flowers as Pond Lilies, Camelias, etc.

Many persons use single wax, and by inserting a very thin muslin between two sheets, and pressing them firmly together, thus make the leaves stronger and better able to endure hard moulding.

The wax now comes all prepared in sheets, and the colors most needed in sheet-wax are White, Yellow and Green. More white wax is used than other colors in making flowers, as most of the other colors can be produced by using the dry colors upon the white wax. These colors come prepared in bottles ready for use.

Some persons may not be successful in coloring the wax, and so there are many other colors in sheet-wax—such as Violet, Pink,

Crimson, Blue, Scarlet, etc., etc.—but these are seldom required, as almost any person of ingenuity and skill can do what coloring is necessary.

LIST OF MATERIALS.

The articles used in making wax flowers are as follows:

White sheet-wax, double and single: green wax, in two shades, for the upper and under parts of the leaf, and it is well also to have two shades of yellow wax.

A pair of fine pointed scissors, thin in the blade, for cutting the wax.

A stiff brush for polishing leaves which have a polished surface—such as the Camelia leaf.

Two or three small sable brushes, for placing the color evenly on the leaves.

Two or three modeling pins for moulding the petals.

Three sizes of wire.

A bottle of gum-water, which one can make by dissolving a little gum arabic in water.

Some pulverized arrow-root for blooming the petals.

It is well enough to have a small palette and palette knife to mix the colors with; but these can be dispensed with, and a common knife used on a plate or other hard substance.

Small saucers or bits of china can be used for the colors.

The colors really necessary for the work are: Carmine, French Ultramarine and Prussian Blue, one or two shades of Chrome Yel· low, Chinese or Flake White, Burnt Sienna and Crimson Lake.

GENERAL DIRECTIONS.

In cutting the petals or leaves out of wax, it will be necessary to frequently dip the scissors in water, so that the wax will not adhere to them. Be careful always to keep the scissors free from wax, as, you will thus get a smoother edge, which is very essential.

There are cutters now made for the petals and other parts of nearly all flowers. These save much time and labor, but many do not wish to go to the expense of procuring them, and I therefore give directions for cutting with scissors, as that is the most common way.

There are also stamens come in bunches all prepared for use, but I shall describe how these may be made and save expense:

Take sewing cotton and cut into suitable lengths, and stiffen with a little starch or gum-water. When perfectly dry dip in melted wax. Form the anthers by cutting tiny bits of wax, rolling between the fingers, and pressing on the end of the stamen ; paint with gum-water, and then dip in yellow powder to imitate the pollen. Many flowers require the stamens to be made of wax. This is done by cutting a piece of thin wax into fine shreds and painting with the gum-water—after which the yellow powder is used.

Having selected the materials for work, the next thing is how to obtain the correct pattern of the parts of the flower you wish to imitate. This is done by carefully taking apart the flower and counting the petals, and laying together such as are first taken from the flower, and so on, until you have the different sizes, and the number of each, in separate places. Then cut out of stiff paper a pattern of each size, and mark on one side of the pattern the number you may wish to cut. Also number the sizes 1, 2, 3, etc.—No. 1 being the size nearest the centre of the flower. When cutting, lay the paper pattern or petal you wish to cut on the wax, then carefully cut away the wax from around the pattern. If your wax should trouble you by cracking, warm it a little by the fire.

APPLE BLOSSOM.

I have chosen this beautiful little flower as my first lesson because it is so simple in construction.

Cut five petals, the shape of No. 2 in the diagram, out of thick white wax. When this is done bloom them with a mixture of flake white and arrow-root, slightly tinged with pink. This is done by laying the petal of wax in the palm of the left hand, and, with one of the small brushes, going over it on both sides, being careful not to have the bloom or paint touch that part of the petal which is to go on the stem, as the paint prevents the wax from adhering. After the petals are all bloomed, mould each by laying it in the palm of the left hand, using one of the large modeling pins, carefully moulding the edges, so they will be thin and have a crinkly look ; then give a graceful curve or hollow to the centre of the petal with the round end of the modeling pin. The

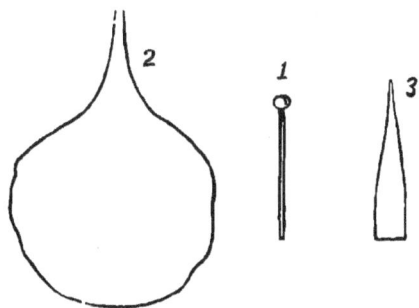

petal should be more deeply shaded in some parts than in others. This can only be done perfectly by having a flower to imitate, or by recollection of the peculiar shading of nature in this flower.

To make up the flower, take a piece of wire, cover it with green wax. This is done by cutting a narrow strip of wax and placing the wire on it, closing the wax over the wire, and then twirling it between the thumb and finger until it is smooth and round. Mould a tiny piece of white wax at one end of the wire for the seed-cup, press around this the twelve stamens, cut like diagram No. 1, which are made thus: Cut finely a piece of white sheet-wax into shreds and dip the ends in gum-water, afterwards dip them into yellow chrome, which is to give the effect of pollen. After these have been firmly pressed to the little seed-cup, then put the five petals at equal distances around the stamens, allowing them to curl and twist carelessly one over the other, as in nature; cut five little pieces, like diagram No. 3, out of the palest green wax, and place them around the seed-cup, so that their points can be seen between the petals; mould them carefully and neatly about the stem, and then wash the stem in gum-water and sprinkle a little arrow-root over it.

In making up a cluster of these flowers the centre stem should be painted with a little brown.

The opening flowers should be more darkly colored than those fully blown.

POND LILY.

I have chosen this beautiful flower for my second lesson, because with very little care, it can be imitated with great exactness.

Extra thick wax must be used for all the petals of this flower. The stamens, which are irregular in size, are to be cut of thick light yellow or cream-colored wax. The form is given them by drawing through them the small end of the modeling pin, after which they are dipped in chrome yellow to give the appearance of being rough with pollen.

Make the stem of stout wire covered with light green wax, cover one end with light yellow or cream-colored wax about the size of a small cherry, indent this with the small end of the modeling pin so as to divide the seed-cup into indentures, then color it with the deepest shade of chrome.

The petals will need careful moulding to give the thin appearance necessary to the edge of the petal. After the edges are moulded thin, draw the head of the large modeling pin through the petal to give the proper curve to it.

All the petals should be bloomed or coated over with flake white and arrow-root mixed, rubbed on dry to give a sparkling whiteness, which is one of the peculiarities of the flower.

There are five different sizes of petals to this flower, with eight petals of each size, the forms of which will be seen by the accompanying diagram.

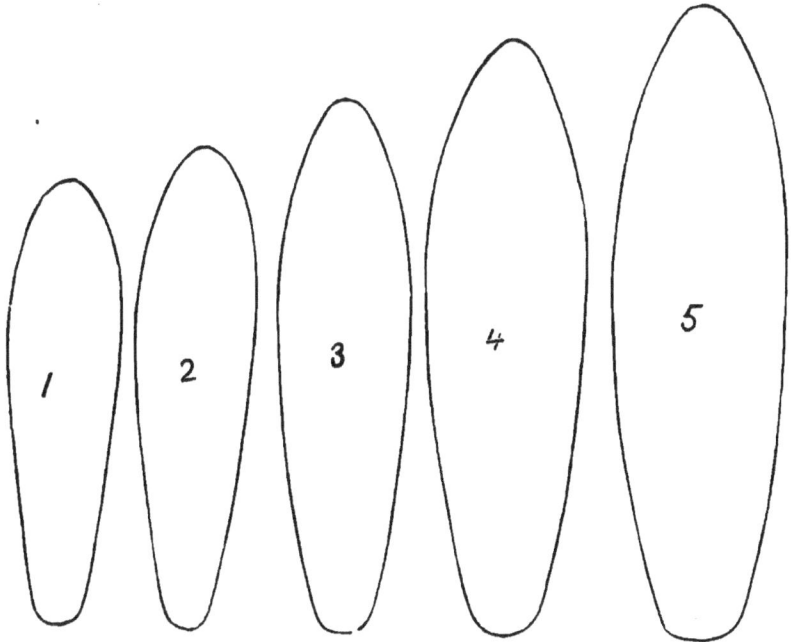

When you are ready to put the flower together, begin with the stamens; the smallest should be moulded on first, and should bend toward the centre, over the seed-cup; each row of stamens should spread a little more, until the last row should almost bend backwards.

Then the smallest petals should be put on—mould first a petal on one side of the seed-cup and another directly opposite—then fill up the spaces, and continue this until all the petals are arranged, a petal always against the space left.

The four outside petals are of green, lined with white wax, tinted with a pale shade of pink at the points. The points of those on the outside should be a dark olive green, shading off to a light yellowish green towards the stem. It is well to have a flower always at hand when you are making one, as you will then easily see how the petals are arranged and the outside petals tinted. Use the coloring matter rather dry, but mix a small portion of gum-water with it to prevent its rubbing off in the process of moulding.

The calyx, or outside petals, are the most difficult part of the flower, and may try the artistic skill of the pupil; but with patience and following Nature, no difficulty will be experienced.

The bud is on a like foundation as the flower, only that it is not necessary to have stamens, and only a few white petals to show through the green calyx, which should almost close over them.

When the flower and bud are finished, give a thin coating of gum-water to the stem and seed-cup, applied with a small sable brush.

Pond lilies are very pretty arranged on a stand, under a glass shade, which comes for the purpose. The bottom of the stand has a mirror, on which the lilies rest, and which reflects them, giving somewhat the appearance of being in water. Four pond lilies, three buds and a few leaves make a very handsome group.

THE FUCHSIA.

There are many varieties of this flower, but if the construction and coloring of one is given, any other can be as easily imitated.

Cut from double white wax four pieces like the pattern marked No. 1 in the diagram, and four of No. 2. Then, to make the centre or pistil, take a fine wire, cover it with white wax, making a little roll at the end, which you should indent with the modeling pin.

Then cut from white wax the stamens, which are eight in number, roll these until they are smooth and round, and then form the anthers at the end of each stamen by doubling the wax over at the end once or twice. The stamens and pistil should be tinted with a pale shade of pink. The anthers or ends of the stamens with a darker shade, and the round end of the pistil tinted with pale green. After your stem has been prepared, by making at the proper distance on the stem a roll of white wax to fasten the petals on, fasten to this the pistil, and then press around this the eight stamens. Now give the proper curve or roundness to the petals marked No. 1 and color them on both sides with carmine, making the edges of the petals darker than the centre; arrange these around the stem, previously made ready, leaving the stamens protruding about an inch. Then mould the outside petals or calyx, marked No. 2, which are left white, using a little arrowroot to give a bloom to the petal as in Nature. Be careful not to let this extend to that part of the leaf which is to be attached

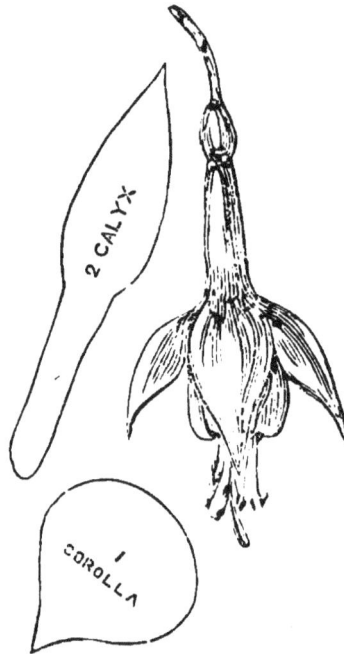

to the stem, as the wax will not adhere when moulding. Put these on, one opposite the other, and let them curl back a little, as it gives a more natural appearance to the flower. And finally fix on the seed vessel, which should be of dark green. The buds you can easily make without special direction; there is no need of the pistil or stamens with a small bud, but a half-blown bud would need them, only they would not protrude as much as in the full-blown flower.

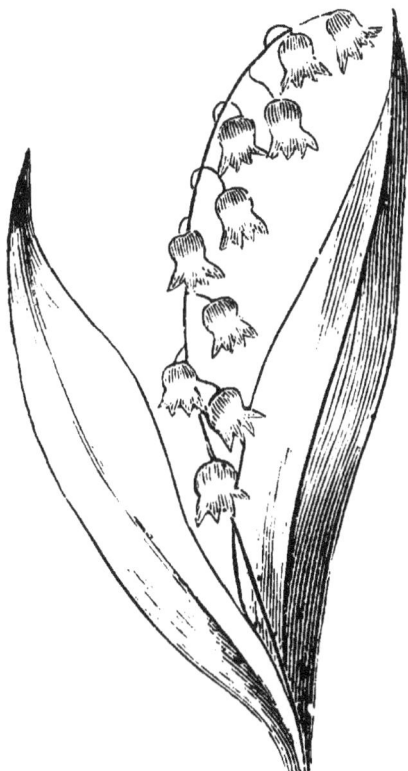

LILY OF THE VALLEY.

This little flower, which is a great favorite, is easily imitated, but it is better for the pupil to have a cutter for this flower.

Cut of double white wax and bloom with a little arrowroot. Mould the flower with the small modeling pin so as to give it somewhat the curved appearance of the inside of a bell, then place it on the round end of one of the small modeling pins and carefully fasten together the seam, holding it near the fire so that the wax will be more easily moulded. The little points around the edge of the bell should now be turned outward, and given form with the small modeling pin or by the use of the fingers.

The stem should be made of the finest wire, on the end of which you fix the pistil and stamens, which are very small, and made of pale yellow wax, painted with chrome yellow to imitate the pollen. Now pass the wire through the top of the bell, drawing it tight to the top and pressing it very carefully at the top of the bell. The stem should be covered afterward with light green wax.

The buds are made the same as the flower, except that the little points on the edge of the flower turn inward, which gives it a closed appearance.

After you have made enough for a stalk of them, arrange by placing the smallest buds and the flowers least opened first, the others following on either side, imitating the arrangement observed in the natural flower.

BLUSH ROSE.

I have chosen this rose because it is one that can be easily obtained and the directions I give for this will equally apply to any other, except, of course, the number and form of the petals and the coloring, which must be copied always from the flower you wish to imitate. In the general directions you will find how the pattern should be obtained and it is not necessary to repeat.

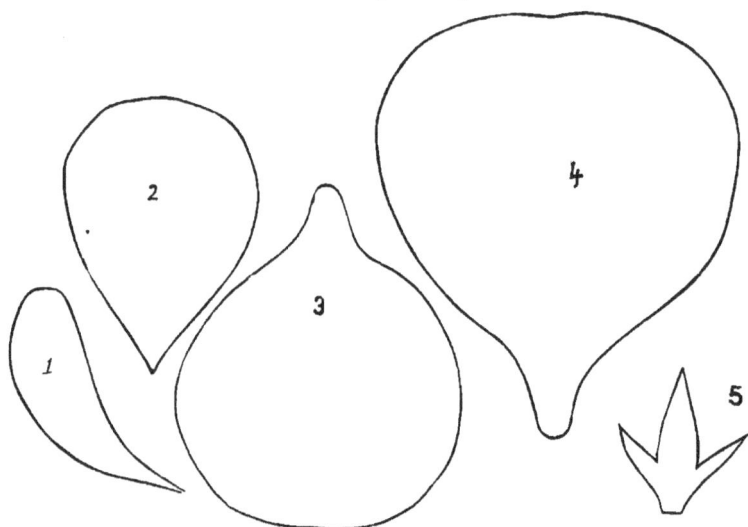

The petals are of four sizes, as per diagram. Of Nos. 1 and 2 cut twenty each, of Nos. 3 and 4 cut sixteen each. After this is done mix thoroughly a little Chinese or flake white with a lesser quantity of arrowroot, and carefully apply it to both sides of the leaf with a camel's-hair brush. When they are all bloomed or painted, and put in order as they are to be placed on the flower, the petals are to be moulded. Hold the petal in the palm of the left hand, using the modeling pin with the right hand. The smaller petals, No. 1, will be crinkled with the small end of the modeling pin. The other petals are moulded with the large end of the pin, rolling from the edge of the petal towards its centre, so as to produce the roundness necessary for the formation of the leaf; sometimes pressing the thumb in the centre of the leaf will give the effect needed. After the leaves have all been thus treated, a little lake and carmine should be added to the mixture before used, giving it a pale shade of pink. The smallest petals should be the deepest in color, the second size less, and so on, until the outer leaves should have but the faintest tinge of pink. Care should be taken that the color should never come to the base of the petal, or the part that moulds on the stem, as it will not adhere when making up.

To make the rose, take a strong wire the length you wish your stem to be, roll a bit of white wax on the end, turn the end over double, and then put on another piece of wax, pressing it between the thumb and finger, and rolling it until it forms a kind of cone the size of a small cherry. It must not be too large or it will make the seed-cup look awkward when finished. Now press on the stamens, which should be made of double white wax cut into shreds about half an inch in length, their points dipped in gum-water, and then into yellow powder to imitate the pollen. The stamens should number about twenty, and some of them should mingle with the smallest or crushed petals of the flower. These should now be pressed on the seed-cup. Some should bend inward, others stand upright, some bend back, and some should be more crushed and crinkled than others, in every way copying Nature. Now take five of No. 2 and one of No. 3, arrange them in a kind of nest, the larger petal upon the outside, press these firmly together at the base of the petals, and then upon the seed-cup or cone, press on three clusters of petals in the same way. This gives the cup-like appearance noticed in the centre of this flower. Then press the remainder of the No. 3 and No. 4 on singly, so as to blend with those already on. The outside petals should turn away gracefully from the other petals, and should exhibit freedom and boldness of form. Much of this is attained by manipulating the leaves with the fingers. The calyx or little green leaves, cut like No. 5, are of light green double wax. Mould with small modeling pin, and place in proper position at equal distances around the seed-cup. If the seed-cup has lost its form in putting on the leaves, it must have any extra accumulation of wax now removed.

The stem should be covered with green wax before the rose is made, and this is done by cutting the wax into narrow strips, laying the wire through the strips of wax and pressing the wax around the wire, then rolling it between the thumb and finger until the stem is smooth and round. It is always well to cover the stem before the flower is commenced.

Make the buds by rolling up some wax in the form of a small cone, then press on five or six pink petals around the cone and place the calyx or five divisions of green around this, having them nearly meet at the top.

For leaves, see description of "How to make wax leaves."

CARNATION PINK.

This beautiful flower, which we all know very well, is a great acquisition to a bouquet, or a group of them alone is very pretty in a small vase for the table.

It can be easily procured from almost any garden, and the patterns obtained in the same way as before described, by carefully taking the flower to pieces. When this is done, it will be found that the petals are of four sizes, as seen in the diagram.

Cut from white wax, four each of Nos. 2 and 3, of Nos. 4 and 5 cut twelve each. A ragged edge must be given each petal with the scissors, and the form also given each by moulding, before the painting or coloring is done. Mould the upper part of the petal in the centre with the large modeling pin, afterward lay the stem of the pin through the long part of the petal on the opposite side from which you have been modeling, so that it will turn the petal back a little, then with the thumb and finger pinch the petal, so as to form the little ridge seen in the petal. Now paint each side of the petals with carmine made moist with a little weak gum-water, and paint heavier in some parts than others, adding a little lake, as almost every shade is to be found in these flowers. Only the round part of the petals must be painted.

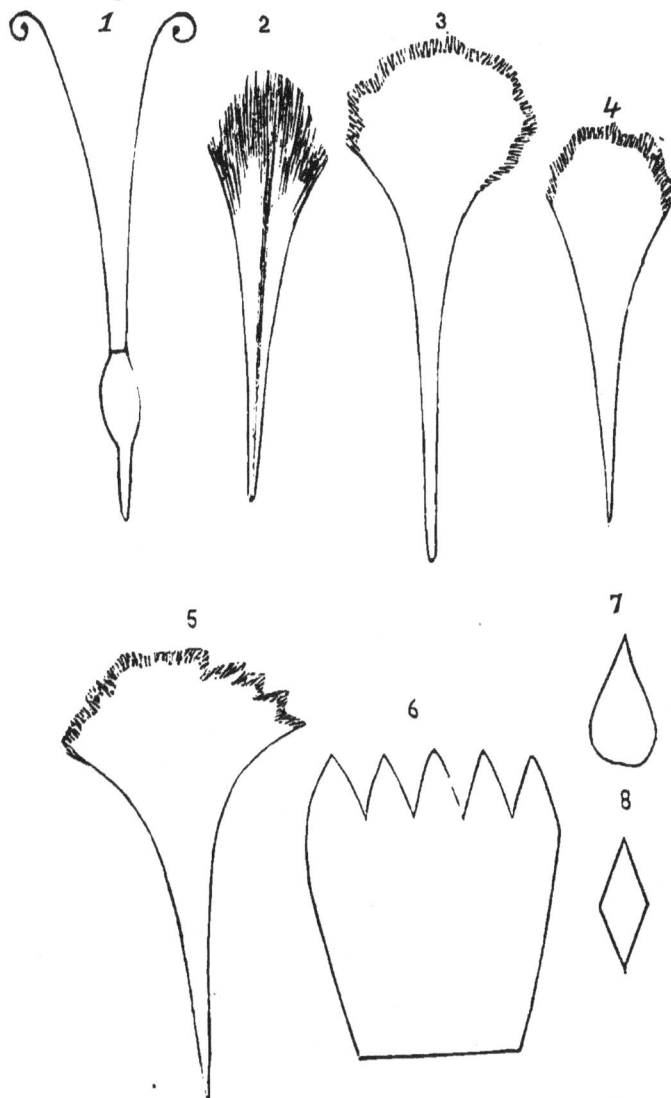

If the petal have lost its form in coloring, you must again carefully form it either with the modeling pin or fingers. To produce the velvety appearance natural to this flower, put on a second shade of color while the first color is stilldamp.

To make the foundation, take a strong piece of wire and on this place the anthers or horns, as seen in diagram. These are cut from thick white wax in narrow shreds, and are about an inch and a half long. Mould around these a small piece of green wax, pressing it into the form and size of a large grain of wheat.

Now press on the petals, placing the smallest first, and avoiding anything like regularity or stiffness in their arrangement, then follow with the other sizes. Some should stand upright, others bend backwards, and all should carelessly curl and twist one over the other. When these are all pressed firmly around the stem, cut out the calyx from thick pale green wax, like No. 6 in diagram, press this around the lower part of the flower, and then finish the base with small green leaves cut like Nos. 7 and 8 in the diagram. Cut two of each. First press on the two of No. 7, one opposite the other, and fill in the spaces with the two cut like No. 8. When these are all nearly pressed to the calyx, let the tops of each of these little leaves stand out from the base of the calyx. It gives a very good effect to this flower to cut two narrow leaves of pale green and fasten to the stem. These should have a little blooming of arrowroot to give the whitish appearance noticeable in the foliage of this flower.

The opening buds should be formed with five or six petals, on a foundation made similar to the one described for the flower, and the outside finished in the same way with the calyx and small green leaves.

The closed buds can be made of a solid piece of wax, with the calyx of green to cover it, pressed together at the point.

A white carnation can be made in the same way described above, the blooming or painting of the white petals to be done with flake white and arrowroot in equal parts mixed.

THE PANSY.

This little flower, which is a favorite with all, may possibly tax somewhat the patience of the pupil, as the coloring is rather difficult.

The one I have selected for my lesson is one which is quite common and therefore easy to obtain, the colors being purple and pale straw-color.

Cut all the petals from white wax, one petal like No. 1, two each of Nos. 2 and 3.

After these are all carefully cut, they should be moulded before coloring. Mould the edges into the requisite thinness, then give as much as possible the natural roundness to the petal. Make a purple by using carmine and Prussian blue with a little lake added, mix these colors well together with a very little weak gum-water. This color should be used moist and applied with a camel's-hair brush to the petals marked No. 3.

Take the petals marked Nos. 1 and 2 and bloom them with a mixture of flake white and arrowroot, with a little chrome added to give it the palest straw color. Paint the edges with the purple, and with the finest point possible of a small brush vein the centre of these petals. This must be done very accurately, and veined downward from the centre.

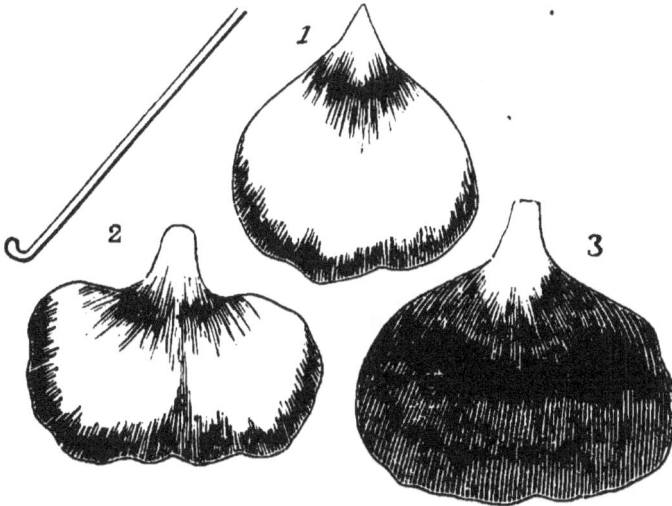

There should be a darker shade of gold color added to the centre of the petals, but the coloring can only be done well by following the natural flower, and ought never to be attempted unless the pupil has one at hand.

To make up the flower take a piece of wire, and to the end press a small piece of light green wax about as large as a grain of rice. This should be quite small at the end, as it is for the pistil of the flower. When this is ready, press on the lower petal No. 1, and then press on either side of this the petals marked No. 2 to form the sides of the flower, after which the purple petals for the upper part of the flower should be added.

When these are all on, curve them back according to the natural flower and add the calyx, which is cut in five small divisions out of light green wax.

The flowers should be grouped or arranged as seen in Nature.

WAX LEAVES.

To make wax leaves, the first thing necessary is to get a pattern of the leaf you wish to imitate. This you can do by cutting a pattern from the natural leaf if you have one at hand, or you can take a pattern from the metal mould which comes for every kind of leaf.

Prepare the wire for the stem the length you desire, cover this with green wax, which is done thus:—cut the wax in narrow strips not more than an eighth of an inch wide, lay the wire upon the wax and press the wax together over it, then twirl it between the thumb and finger until it is smooth and round. If the scissors should trouble you by sticking to the wax, dip them in water, or if the wax should trouble you by cracking, hold it for a moment by the fire.

The wires for individual leaves do not require to be more than six inches in length usually.

Take two sheets of green wax, one dark and the other light, for the upper and under sides of the leaf, lay them one upon the other, press slightly together, so they will not slip—then lay on the pattern of the leaf you wish to imitate, and with the scissors cut away the wax from around the pattern, then slip the wire up through the centre of the leaf you have cut, between the layers of wax, and carefully press the wax about the wire so it will keep its place.

Dip the mould in water to prevent the wax from sticking to it, then lay the leaf of wax—the dark wax down on what seems to be the under side of the leaf mould, or the convex side. Press it firmly and equally into the mould, and be careful not to press the stem too hard, as it may break the wax about the stem. When this is done lift the leaf up by the stem, and you will then have the impression of the lines or veins of the mould upon the leaf.

Almost all leaves require a little painting to make them look like the natural leaf. This is done with Prussian blue and chrome yellow, with a little touch of burnt sienna applied with a small sable brush.

If the leaf should have a glossy appearance, as a camelia leaf, for instance, polish the leaf with a soft brush.

Some leaves, like the geranium, require a covering of down after the coloring or painting—for this use a little arrowroot.

Some persons succeed better to use the paint moist, others prefer the dry colors. If you wish your colors moist, use a little weak gum-water to mix them with, and apply to the leaf with a stiff brush.

It is not necessary to have a different sized mould for every leaf—for instance, you may wish to make a cluster of rose leaves, some may be much larger than others, the largest leaf mould will answer for the smaller leaves. It is more convenient to have the different sizes, but not necessary.

VINES OF IVY.

VINES OF IVY are very pretty, and are made to imitate Nature so accurately, that a very close examination is necessary to detect them from the real vines. They are useful for twining around pictures, where it would be difficult to make the ivy plant grow.

Make the leaves of different sizes by the general directions given above; after your leaves are all finished, take a long wire, the length you wish your vine, cover it with wax and place one of the smallest leaves on the end of it, then press on the other leaves, first on one side of the stem and then upon the other, rolling the stem between the thumb and finger, so it may be smooth and round. No special directions are necessary in regard to placing the leaves, only do not place them too closely; but remember to faithfully imitate Nature, and thus achieve success.

AUTUMN LEAVES.

The same general directions are to be observed in making autumn leaves that I have given above.

To make a maple leaf, take two sheets of bright yellow wax. press them slightly to prevent their slipping, and then cut out the leaf. after which insert the stem previously prepared between the two layers of wax and press firmly, so that the stem will retain its place in the centre of the leaf.

Now take a brush with dry carmine and color the leaf in places, rubbing and softening the color so that it will not look hard upon the leaf; paint both sides of the leaf, leave some very bright spots on the face of the leaf.

If you wish to have other colors with the red and yellow—for there is sometimes a great variety of colors on one leaf—use the other coloring matter in the same way, being careful always to have one color blend softly into the other. Sometimes a leaf needs to have a brown tinge, for this use burnt scinna; if green, use Prussian blue and chrome yellow mixed.

After the leaf is painted press it into the convex side of the mould, which must always be dipped in water before being used, to prevent the wax from sticking to it. The colors will be wet upon the leaf when you take it from the mould. Shake off any surplus moisture and then lay the leaf aside until dry. It will then be necessary to retouch it with dry color.

Other maple leaves may be made by cutting out of light green wax and using the different colors upon green; you will thus have a larger variety, and a little practice will soon teach you how to use the colors.

Oak leaves are cut out of light green wax. Sumach leaves should be cut of yellow wax and colored with carmine. The stems of all leaves will partake somewhat of the color of the leaf.

Great taste may be displayed in coloring the leaves, for which comparatively few directions can be given. Procure some autumn leaves therefore, the brightest and handsomest you can find, and imitate the coloring. It is not possible to add beauty to any of Nature's works, therefore be careful and faithfully imitate.

WAX CROSSES.

To imitate a marble cross, the first thing necessary will be to procure a wooden cross of suitable dimensions, with two or three steps at its base.

Paint it white, or cover it with fine white paper, being careful that all the edges of the paper are firmly fastened with mucilage.

When this is done, proceed to cover the cross with double white wax, commencing at the base and working upward. using great care that the wax should lay smoothly and be neatly fastened at the edges of the cross, where it should always be joined.

After the cross is finished proceed to ornament, which is done to suit the taste of the operator. The most simple ornamentation is a graceful ivy vine. Make the leaves in precisely the same manner as described elsewhere, only of pure white wax, and use a very fine white silk covered wire for stems.

Have the fingers perfectly clean, and it is well always to take the precaution to roll a bit of wax between the fingers before moulding the leaves or covering the wire for stems—everything depends upon the purity of the work.

Some prefer other kinds of ornamentation; rose leaves and half open rose buds at the base of the cross, and a spray of the same falling gracefully from the arms of the cross is very pretty. Another very graceful vine for this purpose is the passion flower.

When the cross is entirely finished and ornamented, if it is desired to frost it, take a soft camel's-hair brush, and carefully touch the surface of the work with a little thin mucilage and sprinkle with "diamond dust."

AUTUMN LEAF CROSS.

Take a wooden cross the same as heretofore described, paint with gray-colored paint, and while the paint is wet, sand it with gray sand. A few small pieces of rough stone may be dipped in melted wax and sanded in the same way, and laid at the base of the cross.

The wax leaves are then moulded as described in our lesson on making autumn leaves, made into a vine and twined gracefully around the body of the cross and allowed to fall over the arms.

Make the leaves of the vine quite small, and use the larger ones to group around the base of the cross.

The woodbine leaf is very pretty for this use, while the small dark berries belonging to the vine give a pretty contrast of color.

Any small bright leaf made in a graceful vine with some variety of color looks well if arranged with taste.

WAX FRUIT.

A mould of the fruit you wish to imitate must first be obtained. The materials required for the moulds, are plaster of Paris of best quality; a sheet of tin or pasteboard, cut into strips from three to four inches in width; some fine damp sand in a basin; another basin in which to mix the plaster, a knife, some water, and a little oil. Suppose an apple the fruit you wish to model. The first thing to be done is to carefully cover the fruit with oil. When this is done, sink just one-half the apple in the basin of damp sand, placing the stem downward; and after smoothing the sand around it, fix a strip of tin or pasteboard into the sand, making the ends meet, and leaving a margin of an inch or more all around the apple, and a little above the apple. Then mix your plaster with water in a basin until it is a little thicker than cream; pour this mixture of plaster on the apple until it is entirely covered, and let it become perfectly hard or firm before it is handled.

Clean the basin that contained the plaster ready for the next half mould, as the plaster becomes solid so soon.

When the mould is firm enough to handle, remove the whole from the sand, taking off the hoop of tin which encloses the mould and carefully remove the apple from it, shaping the mould with a knife neatly and regularly all around to the exact half of the apple; then pierce two or three holes in the edge of the mould at stated distances, and the first half of the mould is complete.

The other half of the mould is made thus:—oil the edges and holes of the mould thoroughly and replace the apple in the mould, being careful to make all parts perfectly fit. Fix around the mould a strip of the tin or pasteboard, and tie it firmly so it will not slip, then pour the plaster mixture before described upon the apple so as to quite cover it. This must be allowed to set or get firm, and when this is done remove the tin and the mould will now separate; you can then take out the apple and the mould is complete.

Different forms of fruit will require different treatment; as, for instance, a pear will need to be laid on its side, a melon mould will have to be formed of three or four pieces.

Great care must be taken to construct the mould so as to allow the natural fruit to be easily taken out, or else the wax casting could not be removed without breaking. It is best to allow a day or two to pass after making the mould before it is used, that the plaster may become perfectly hard.

Be careful to remove all sand from the fruit before making the last half of the mould.

After the mould has been prepared, the next thing is to form the fruit. The mould must be placed in moderately warm water for a few minutes before using it, so as to prevent the wax from sticking to it.

The wax must be of the best quality of white wax, the same as for flowers. If you have scraps of wax which have been left from making wax flowers they can now be used. The colors used are much the same as in flower modeling.

Melt the wax so it shall be thoroughly heated, but never allow it to boil. If your apple is to be green, use a little Prussian blue and yellow chrome. Stir or mix the coloring matter thoroughly with the wax. Now take the mould from the water and carefully wipe it inside and out; hold one half in the left hand, nearly fill the mould with the melted wax, being careful not to let the wax get on the edge of the mould, then put the other half mould upon it and hold them tightly together, then proceed to turn the mould over and over in the hands. This must be done gently, so that when the wax sets inside, it may be deposited evenly over the surface of the mould. The wax will soon cease to move, and you may then in a few moments place the mould in moderately warm water. Let it stay for a short time and it will then be ready to take apart, when the perfect apple will appear. There may be a slight mark where the halves of the mould join, which can be obliterated in a moment by trimming with a knife and then smoothing with a rag dipped in turpentine.

The apple can now be touched up if desired with a little coloring matter, one side tinted with a little carmine.

The flower end of the apple may be imitated by heating the end of a clove, and sinking it into the apple while the clove is hot; always be careful in doing this not to injure the form of the cast. The stem of the apple can usually be obtained from the natural fruit; if not easily obtained take a wire, dip in melted wax, and color like Nature.

Some small fruits, such as strawberries, raspberries, &c., are formed solid; the two half moulds are tied together, a small aperture made at one end, and the hot wax poured into the mould.

Currants are made on little glass balls of different sizes, with the wire inserted in them; these are dipped in wax colored with carmine.

When a sufficient number have been made, they must be tied together in a cluster and painted at the end with a little sepia. After this is done they should be varnished.

White currants should be colored a yellowish light green.

Purple grapes are made in much the same way. From three to five dozen glass balls of a purple hue of the size required should be selected; an equal number of stalks should be cut from green silk covered wire, to fit the mouth of the ball. Color the wax with a mixture of lake and Prussian blue; dip one end of the wire into the melted wax and insert that end quickly into the mouth of the ball, and after a moment it will be fixed.

After all the grapes are thus stalked, drop the ball of each into the hot wax and quickly take it out, then turn it round and round, so that any extra wax will settle on the stem; the grapes will then have a covering of wax which represents the real fruit.

The grapes, when finished, should be grouped by tying them together, the smaller ones at the bottom and the larger ones at the top. Sprinkle with a little powder of arrowroot and Prussian blue to impart the bloom of the natural fruit.

White grapes are made the same, only tint the wax with a light yellowish green and bloom slightly with arrowroot.

PRICE LIST OF
WAX FLOWER MATERIALS.

— ● —

BEST SHEET WAX—SIZE, 3¼x5¼.

Single White and all Shades of Green, Yellow, Blue, Buff and Purple, in
    Packages of One Dozen Sheets of one Shade, per package... .... $0 12
One Gross of 12 packages, one color or assortment of above colors.... .... 1 30
    Not less than One Dozen Sheets sent, but they will be assorted at
20c. per Dozen.

Double White, Scarlet, Red, Pink, Carmine, per Dozen Sheets of one
    Shade 0 25
One Gross of 12 Packages of one color or assorted........................ 2 50
One Dozen Assorted Colors................,...................... .... 0 30

Pond Lily Wax—White or Green, per Package of Six Sheets, One Color.. 0 20
Twelve Packages of Six Sheets each, all White or White and part Green.. 2 00
One Package Six Sheets Assorted Colors................................ 0 25

Brass Moulds for Leaves

	A	B	C			A	B	C
	c.	c.	c.			c.	c.	c.
Arbutilon.............each	15	12	—	Ivy ....each	12	10	8
Archarenthus.......... "	15	12	8	Laurestine.............. "	15	12	8
Azalie.................. "	15	12	8	Lilac................... "	20	15	12
Blackberry............. "	15	12	8	Lily of Valley.......... "	15	8	—
Butterfly.............. "	15	12	8	Maple.................. "	35	30	20
Camelia................ "	20	15	—	Oak.................... "	30	25	20
Chresentum............ "	15	12	—	Orange................. "	12	10	--
Cape Jasamin.......... "	15	12	8	Pansey................. "	12	10	--
Cherry................. "	20	15	--	Passion Flower......... "	15	--	--
Chestnut............... "	30	25	15	Pond Lily.............. "	20	15	--
Clemestina............. "	20	15	15	Pyrus Japonica......... "	15	12	8
Currant................ "	12	10	—	Rose................... "	15	12	8
Dogwood............... "	30	15	—	Rose Geranium......... "	10	8	—
Fish Geranium......... "	15	12	--	Strawberry............. "	15	10	8
Fuschia .... "	15	12	8	Salvia................. "	15	10	8
Grape.................. "	30	25	—	Sumac.................. "	10	8	—
Heliotrope............. "	12	10	8	Verbena................ "	12	10	8
Honeysuckle.... ...... "	20	15	12	Violet................. "	15	12	8
Sassafras............... "	30	25	15	Myrtle................. "	15	12	10
Elm.................... "	20	15	..	Woodbine.............. "	20	15	15
Jessamine............. "	10	10	..	Fern.... .... "	30	30	..
Willow................. "	20	15	..	Peach.................. "	25	20	..

TIN AND BRASS CUTTERS.

	cts.		cts.
Rose Geranium.............each.	16	Orange.....................each,	20
Fish Geranium............... "	20	Violet....................... "	15
Pink....................... "	20	Jasamine.................... "	15
Fuschia................. .... "	15	Honeysuckle .... "	15
Camella.................... "	30	Verbena, A................. "	15
Tube Roses................. "	30	Verbena, B................. "	15
Pond Lily.................,.... "	50	Lily of Valley, A .... "	15
Pansey..................... "	30	Lily of Valley, B........... "	15
Rose....................... "	50	Heliotrope, A............... "	15
Dahlia..................... "	40	Heliotrope, B............... "	15
Wisteria................... "	20	Heliotrope C................ "	15
Forget-Me-Not........ .... "	15	Azalia, large .... "	15
Sweet Pea .... "	20	" medium............... "	15
Moss Rose Calyx............ "	15	" small,.............. .... "	15
Quaker Lady................ "	15	Easter Lily................. "	15
Sweet Alysium.............. "	15	Lilac.. .... "	15
Clemintine................. "	15	Hyacinth .... "	15
Wild Rose.................. "	15	Star Flower................. "	15
Narcis..................... "	15		

SEE NEXT PAGE.

EXTRA FINE DRY COLORS.

In Homo Phials. Expressly prepared for Coloring Wax.

Cts.

Burnt Sienna, Burnt Umber, Brilliant Yellow, Chrome Green, No. 1, No. 2
and No. 3, Chrome Yellow, No. 1, No 2 and No. 3, Diamond Dust,
Frostings, Emerald Green, Flake White, Indian Red, Naples Yellow,
Prussian Blue, Raw Sienna, Raw Umber, Rose Pink, Silver White,
Yellow Oohre, Bloom........... .... each 15
Cobalt Blue, Crimson Lake, Lemon Yellow, Purple Lake, Royal Purple,
Scarlet Lake, Vermilion, Rose Madder, No. 1, No. 2 and No. 3, Ultra-
marine Blue, No. 1, No. 2 and No. 3 , ... each 20
Carmine, Magenta, Mauve, Pure Scarlet, Solferino, Violet . ...each 30

Sundries.

Silk Wire, per spool or coil................................... 15
Cotton Wire, " " 10
White Annealed Wire, per spool or coil 10
Green Moss, per bunch 15
Sprig Moss in Envelopes, for Moss Roses............................ .. 5
Stamins, per bunch, any color..................................... 5
Palate Knives for mixing 3 inches 30
" " 3½ " 40
Immortelle Flowers, all colors, per bunch.......................... .. 50
Bristol Poonah Brushes................................. ....each 15
Dusters, Camel's Hair........ ....each 15
Camel's Hair Brushes..each 3
Rosewood Moulding Tools....... ....each 10
Steel Pins........ ....each 10
Ground Arrowroot for Blooming, in ¼ lb. packages 30

	6 in.	8½ in.	9½ in.	12 in.
Wood Crosses...... . ...each	$0 25	$0 40	$0 50	$0 75
Imitation Stone Crosses........ ....each		1 50		2 50

Green Buds and Calyx of Pinks, per doz....... 30
" " Roses, " 10
Worsted Chenelle, any color, per yard.... 10
Silk " " " " 20
"WAX FLOWERS and FRUIT MAKING, WITHOUT A TEACHER,"
a complete book of instructions with illustrations................... 50

The above book is sent free to persons ordering $2.50 worth of wax material.

Plaster Paris Moulds

In great variety, such as for Apples, Pears, Peaches, Lemons, Oranges,
small Vegetables, etc , etc.
Prices of these and like sizes of Fruit, etc., each........ 50
Extra sizes in proportion.
If these moulds are ordered to be sent by mail, 16 cents extra for the common sizes and 25 cents extra for larger sizes, must be sent in addition to price to
pay postage. If any number are ordered at one time it will be better to have
them go by express.

POND LILY STANDS AND SHADES,
With Mirror Complete.

6 in.	7 in.	8 in.	9 in.	10 in.	11 in.	12 in.	13 in.
$1 40	$1 75	$2 00	$2 50	$3 00	$4 00	$4 75	$5 50

The size given is the diameter of the shade. Fifty cents extra is
charged for packing and boxing. The Shades and Stands can only be sent by
express
The price of Stand and Shade of any size, either square or round, for
Crosses, Bouquets of Flowers, etc , will be sent on application, when the size,
(diameter and height)is given.

English Steel Engravings.

We have obtained the Agency of the following English Steel Engravings, and have reduced the prices to one-third the former prices, hoping thereby to obtain for them a large sale:

We send them Post Paid on Receipt of Price.

		SIZE	Our price each.
Protection.	Landseer	12x15	$0 40
Discovery	"	12x15	0 40
Capture	"	12x15	0 40
Mother's Pet	Wilkie	15x12	0 40
Grandma's Darling	"	15x12	0 40
Now I Lay Me Down to Sleep	"	13x11	0 40
Saved	Landseer	16x20	0 40
Off to the Rescue	"	16x20	0 40
Inundation	"	16x20	0 40
Stag at Bay	"	16x20	0 40
Death of the Stag	"	16x20	0 40
Laying Down the Law	"	16x20	0 40
Bolton Abbey	"	16x20	0 40
Midsummer Night's Dream	"	15x20	0 40
Fruit Girl	Wilkie	17x12	0 40
Gleaner	"	17x13	0 40
Pedlar	"	20x16	0 40
Guess My Name	"	20x16	0 40
Farm Yard	Herring	16x20	0 65
Homestead	"	17x20	0 65
Shoeing the Horse	"	20x16	0 65
Feeding the Horse	"	20x16	0 65
The Halt	"	20x16	0 65
Lake Pepin, Upper Mississippi		14x17	0 65
Crossing the Mississippi on Ice		14x11	0 65
Wooding up on the Mississippi		14x18	0 65
Mary Queen of Scots		16x13	0 65
Beatrice Cenci		15x12	0 65
Uranie		15x12	0 65
Raphael		15x12	0 65
Delaware Water Gap		14x17	0 65
Clifty Falls, Madison, Ind		14x17	0 65
Rock River, near Janesville, Wis		14x17	0 65
The Orphans		22x28	1 00
Our Father which Art in Heaven		22x28	1 00
We Praise Thee, O God		22x28	0 60
Vale of Peace		18x23	0 40
The Virgin		19x16	0 50
The Saviour		19x16	0 50
Child's First Prayer		16x19	0 40
The Poor Relations		16x20	0 40
Home from the War		21x27	0 80
Merry Making in Olden Time		21x27	0 70

CHROMOS.

The following list of choice Chromos we are now enabled to send our patrons—by mail, post paid—at the extremely low prices annexed.

	Size.	Price.
" Morning on the Mountains"—Landscape with Sheep	11x26	$ 75
" Midday "—Landscape with Cattle	11x26	75
After celebrated German paintings.		
" A Foggy Morning on the Banks "	14½x25	75
" Off Boars' Head, Hampton Beach, N. H.	14½x25	75
Copies of the much-admired marine views, by D. Weber.		
" Gathering Primroses "	17x22	50
" In the Woods "	17x22	50
From English water colors.		
The Country Stile	11x16	35
English Cottage Scene	11x16	35
The Darling Babe	11x16	35
The Young Navigators	11x16	35
After celebrated water colors by Burket Foster.		
Lincoln	14x17	1 00
Perry's Victory on Lake Erie	16x22	40
Mount of Olives	10x13	25
Garden of Gethsemane	10x13	25
Fruit Piece	13x16	35
Flower Piece	13x16	35
Little Wanderer	12x15	30
Cascade Falls	13x16	30
The Young Hunter	10x13	30
Monarch of the Glen (Stag)	13x16	40
Maternal Affection (Doe and Fawn)	13x16	40
Asking a Blessing	10x12	1 00
Christ Blessing Little Children	10x12	1 00
George and Martha Washington	9x12	each 20
Illuminated Mottoes	9½x25	each 30
" God Bless our Home," "The Lord is my Shepherd," " Praise the Lord."		
Bouquets—1, 2, 3, 4 Set 35c.	8x10	each 10
Attention	8x10	10
God's Acre	8x10	10
Little Domestic	8x10	10
Little Grocer	8x10	10
My Good Brother	8x10	10
Playing Doctor	8x10	10
Monarch	8x10	10
Putnam at the Plow	16x22	40
Cross and Crown	14x18	40
Cross and Flowers	13x16	40
Sharing the Meal	11x14	30

```
Angling .......................................11x14   each  30
How Tall am I.............................. 9x11         10
Just Caught, very fine................. ...  10x13        15
Cross and Flowers..........................  6x8         10
Landscape and Children.....................10x14         30
Easter Cross and Flowers, white ground......10x14       25
```

Choice Landscape Chromos.

We take pleasure in calling the attention of our patrons to the following list of Chromo Landscapes, of American and Foreign subjects: they are executed in the best manner, and are faithful copies of Choice Paintings. They are sent post-paid at the annexed prices, which are less than one-half the usual retail price.

```
St. Goarshausen,.......................Hiller   19x25  $1 50
Comersee............................Hampe     19x25   1 50
Scheveningen..........................Astudin  19x25   1 50
Dachstein Mountains..................Hiller   19x25   1 50
Home of Deer.............................      19x25   1 50
Sunday Afternoon on West Point Road...Eglau   20x27   1 50
Sunset on Lake Mahonk...............   "      20x27   1 50
Scene on Hudson River...............   "      20x27   1 50
West Point Ferry.....................  "      20x27   1 50
Cascade in Alps....................Hampe 19½x27½ 1 50
Cottage on Kochelsee.................  "    19½x27½ 1 50
Via Mala, I.......................Chevalier 19½x27½ 1 50
Gruetli Chapel I ......  ..........   "    19½x17½ 1 50
Eifel Thal...........................      20x27   1 50
Norwegian Coas .................... .... 20x28   1 50
Valley of Wyoming..... ..... ....... 18½x26½ 1 50
Source o" Delaware................... 21½x26½ 1 50
Merl Abbey.......................... . 19x27  1 50
Kochelsee..........................    19x25   1 50
Zillerthal .........................    20x27   1 50
Beatrice Cenci (Head)..............    24x30   1 25
The Snow Storm....................     24x30   1 30
Fruit and Goldfish.......  ........    24x30   1 25
Yo-semite Valley ....... ............14x20   0 35
On the Saco, N. H...................    8½x13  0 30
Lake Chocorua, N. H.................    8½x13  0 30
Autumn on the Kenebeck, Me............  8½x13  0 30
```

The following Chromos will be sent only in sets, as per list below:

```
Eight assorted Landscapes.................5½x8 per set, 60
    Home with the Flock   |   Off the English Coast
    Pass of St. Gottard   |   Bringing Home the Cows
    The Horseback Party   |   Mount Cenis
    Theobaldi Chapel      |   In the Andes
```

Perforated Card Board

Mottoes for Embroidery.

These Mottoes are printed with a light tint on the card board in such a manner as to make it very easy for any one to make the embroidery, and when made either with silk or worsted, they are very handsome and suitable for framing. We give a list below.

SIZE 8½ x 21¼.

Price 15 cents post-paid.

1 Praise the Lord.
2 Welcome.
3 Pray Without Ceasing.
4 Lead us not Into Temptation
5 The Lord is my Shepherd.
6 In God we Trust.
7 God Bless Our Home.
8 Faith, Hope and Charity.
9 Learn to do Good.
10 Nearer my God to Thee.
11 Give us this Day our Daily Bread.
12 Love One Another.
13 Home, Sweet Home.
14 He Leadeth Me.
15 No Cross, No Crown.
16 God is Love.
18 The Lord Will Provide.
19 Rock of Ages Cleft for Me.
21 Jesus Loves Me.
22 Simply to Thy Cross I Cling.
23 Remember Me.
24 Hallowed be Thy Name.
25 God Bless Our Daily Bread.
26 No Place Like Home.
27 I Need Thee every Hour.
28 Welcome Home.

29 With Joy We Greet You.
31 Sweet Rest in Heaven.
32 Christ is Risen,
33 Thou art my Hope.
35 Friendship, Love and Truth.
36 I Know that my Redeemer Liveth.
37 Thy Will be Done.
40 I am the Bread of Life.
41 Watch and Pray.
43 Do Right and Fear Not.
45 Kindness Makes Friends.
46 Obey Your Parents.
47 Onward and Upward."
48 Labor has sure Reward.
49 Knowledge is Power.
51 Walk in Love.
52 Forget me not.
55 God Bless our School.
60 The Old Oaken Bucket.
63 Be True in Heart.
64 Thine is the Kingdom.
65 Wisdom is Strength.
66 Charity Never Faileth,
78 Merry Christmas,
79 Happy New Year.
80 Honor thy Father and thy Mother.

SIZE 8½ x 10½.

Price 10 cents post-paid.

God Bless Our Home.
Simply to Thy Cross I Cling.
Home, Sweet Home.
Blessed are the Pure in Heart.
Welcome Home.
I Need Thee every Hour.
My Faith Looks up to Thee.
Serve the Lord with Gladness.
Thou God Seest Me.

There is no Place Like Home.
Love Rest and Home.
Hold the Fort.
The Lord will Provide.
Heaven is my Home.
Cling to Jesus.
Thy Will be Done.
Give us this Day our Daily Bread,

We have also a variety of *SMALLER MOTTOES.* Samples of which will be sent for 5c. each.

Patterns for Book Markers, with various mottoes and designs, five for 10 cents.

J. L. PATTEN & CO., 162 William St., New York.

READ THIS!

The Package of Decalcomanie, which we send for **50** cents, contains an assortment of **100** large and small pictures, put up more particularly to please and amuse the little folks. They are prepared ready for use, and if the directions which accompany each package are followed, no trouble will be experienced in transferring them. The small dot near one of the top corners, or a pencil line across the top of many of the pictures, indicates the position they are designed to occupy.

These pictures are something delightful to young and old for amusement, instruction and for embellishing various articles about the house. Merely as a pastime it is a most charming occupation for the young, while it cultivates the taste and gives them an appreciation for the beautiful.

We are also putting up the same in **$1**, **$2** and **$5** packages, containing a much better variety and larger number of pictures than we send in our smaller packages.

We enclose you our Catalogue—the prices are per sheet. We do not send less than one-fourth of a sheet of a kind. We believe, however, that our one dollar or two dollar boxes will give better satisfaction than the same amount that you would select from our catalogue. In ordering the above packages say "prepared" to distinguish them from our Ladies' Boxes. For directions see last part of the last page of this book.

DECALCOMANIE BOXES FOR LADIES.

In addition to the packages of Decalcomanie which we put up for the amusement of children and the family circle, and which you will find noticed above, we are putting it up in boxes expressly for the use of ladies and others who desire only pictures of good size and of the best quality for ornamentation of all kinds. These boxes will contain pictures of ferns, moss roses and buds, Easter morning crosses, several kinds of Autumn leaves in groups, exquisite flower pieces, heads, landscapes, animals, groups of figures, etc., etc. We put this quality up in **$1**, **$2** and **$5** boxes. They are not "prepared" but are to be put on with varnish. Each box contains instructions and brushes but no varnish, as we are not allowed to send it by mail. Any quick drying varnish will answer, however, and this can be obtained at any drug or paint store in the country at a trifling expense. Each picture is numbered so that you can afterwards order sheets of the same if you wish. By referring to the catalogue you will see the number of pictures on a sheet and the price per sheet. Not less than one-fourth of a sheet of a kind sent. The plain or uncovered pictures are best for lamp-shades, porcelain, china, glassware, or for transparencies, but not so good for dark grounds. The most of those numbered in our catalogue with an " m " after the numeral can be sent uncovered if desired; the other numbers cannot be so sent.

For directions see first part of the last page of this book.

We do not promise the same number of pictures in these as in our other boxes, as they are larger and of finer quality, but in putting them up we shall be governed by the same liberality which has always characterized our dealings, and which has enabled us so uniformly to give satisfaction. In ordering these boxes please say "for ladies."

☞ We should feel greatly under obligations to any of our correspondents who will distribute some of our books to their friends and acquaintances, and at the same time speak a good word for our goods; and we shall be glad to furnish the books for that purpose; or if they know of any person out of employment they will do both them and us a favor by calling their attention to our goods as first-rate articles of merchandise to sell. We will send our catalogue, together with samples of Decalcomanie, free and post-paid, to any one whose name and address is furnished us.

Address,

J. L. PATTEN & CO.,

162 William St., New York.

For terms see bottom of title page

ARTICLES
THAT EVERYBODY WANTS.
SENT POST PAID ON RECEIPT OF PRICE.

————◆•————

	$ cts
1 doz. Faber Pencils, good quality.....................	0 25
" " " with rubber tips...................	0 40
1 gross English steel pens, warranted to give satisfaction..	1 00
1 box Stationery—2 quires paper, 2 packages envelopes..	0 50
" Initial stationery, 1 quire paper, 1 package envelopes, two tints of paper—any letter................	0 35
" Imported stationery, 1 quire paper, 1 package envelopes, rep paper—very handsome..............	1 00
1 package (50) blank Bristol board, or satin enamel, cards, for address cards......................	0 25
1 Magnifying glass, single lens	0 50
" " double lens........	1 00
1 Spy glass—good clear glass and constructed on scientific principles.....................................	1 00
1 Gem microscope—100 diameters, 10,000 areas, reveals eels in vinegar, and many other objects in nature not visible to the unassisted eye....................	1 50
1 Watch charm, with microscopic glass, views of cities, streets, portraits, &c....	0 25
1 Watch charm, with compass and magnetic needle......	0 25
" chain, leather and steel.....................	0 35
" ' steel.........................	0 35
" " imitation gold, for lady or gentleman, elegant pattern...................................	1 00
" chain, plated with pure gold	2 00
1 pair cuff buttons, imitation gold.....................	0 50
" " plated with gold....................	1 00
1 Finger ring............................. 25c., 30c. &	1 00
1 set Gents' studs for bosom fronts, 3 in a set..........	0 75
1 Ladies' bosom pin, imitation gold, elegant pattern......	1 00
" ', plated with gold.................	2 00
1 pair ear drops to match .... 1 00 &	2 00
1 doz. fine Stereoscopic Views......................	1 50
1 Spy Glass, very fine acromatic Glasses, three slides.....	3 00
1 doz. Sewing Machine Needles for any standard machine	0 50
1 Perforated Initial Embroidery pattern letter for hdkfs..	0 10
1 Initial Letter for Pillow Shams, either for Embroidery or Braiding..	0 25
1 Corner Piece for Pillow Shams, " " " ..	0 30
1 Centre Piece for Pillow Shams, " " " ..	0 50

J. L PATTEN & CO.,
162 William St., New York.

Assorted Sheets Decalcomanie.

No.	DESCRIPTION.	No. of pcs. on sheet.	Per sht. $ cts.
1..	Landscape, oval (Sea Scenes), 2½x3..	25	60
8..	Birds, assorted, small, 1½x2...............	54	60
9..	Game Cocks, 4x5.........................	12	1 00
11..	Comic Heads, small.......................	88	60
12..	Corner Scrolls, gilt and shaded............	12	25
15..	Comic Heads, medium.....................	40	60
19..	Scrolls, long, gilt and shaded, ¾x2½........	55	25
20..	Landscapes, oval, 5x6½.....................	4	80
25..	" " with border, 3½x4½......	9	70
27..	Borders, gilt and shaded, ½x16.............	12	25
29..	" " " ¾x16............	17	25
32..	Bouquets of Flowers and Fruit, round, 3½x3½	12	60
33..	Bouquets of Flowers, upright, 2x2.........	48	60
45..	Chinese Figures, assorted, 1½x2½...........	21	70
46..	" Scenes, rich and pale gilt.........	15	40
50..	Fruit-piece, large oval, 9½x15½............	1	70
51..	Ladies' Portraits........................	16	70
52..	Fancy Scenes, 3x4.........................	12	70
55..	Fancy Scenes, oval upright, 3x4...........	14	70
70..	Swiss Heads..............................	60	70
87..	Scroll, long gilt and colored, ½x4...........	44	35
88..	Landscapes, oval, 2x3.....................	18	70
90..	Flower-piece, large oval, 9½x15½...........	1	70
94..	Military Figures, French..................	40	55
96..	Corners, red and gold, different sizes.......	36	40
102..	Bouquets, oval, 3x4.......................	16	70
103..	Rosette, with corners, red and gold........	5	20
107..	Shields and Scrolls for Carriages, assorted..	31	70
108..	Scrolls, red and gold, 1¼x3¼....	28	25
111..	Groups of Birds, with nest, 7½x10½........	2	70
113..	" " " flowers, assorted....	24	55
116..	Flower-pieces, small, ¾x1...............	204	55
120..	Bouquets, oval, 3x5.......................	9	60
121..	Birds on Branches, small, assorted.........	68	60
122..	" " " "	28	60
123..	Flowers, very small.......................	432	60
129..	Bouquets, upright, 1½x2..................	72	60
130..	Flowers and Fruit-pieces, 4x5½...........	8	80
134..	Medallions, with Portraits, round, 1½x1½...	63	70
135..	" " oval, 1½x2......	50	70
139..	Ladies' Portraits, small oval, 1¼x1½........	72	70
141..	Bouquets of Fruit, large, 10½x13...........	1	60
143..	Heads, antique, small.....................	280	60
150..	Ladies' Heads, small......................	180	70
151..	Bouquets of Flowers, round, 6x6...........	6	1 00
153..	Military Figures, German..................	40	55

www.ingramcontent.com/pod-product-compliance
Lightning Source LLC
Chambersburg PA
CBHW021457090426
42739CB00009B/1759